7 THINGS THAT MAKE YOU LOVE OR HATE SUCCESS

Why your success never works
out the way you plan

Gurpreet Kaur Chawla

Chennai • Bangalore

CLEVER FOX PUBLISHING
Chennai, India

Published by CLEVER FOX PUBLISHING 2023
Copyright © Gurpreet Kaur Chawla 2023

All Rights Reserved.
ISBN: 978-93-56484-82-5

This book has been published with all reasonable efforts taken to make the material error-free after the consent of the author. No part of this book shall be used, reproduced in any manner whatsoever without written permission from the author, except in the case of brief quotations embodied in critical articles and reviews.

The Author of this book is solely responsible and liable for its content including but not limited to the views, representations, descriptions, statements, information, opinions and references ["Content"]. The Content of this book shall not constitute or be construed or deemed to reflect the opinion or expression of the Publisher or Editor. Neither the Publisher nor Editor endorse or approve the Content of this book or guarantee the reliability, accuracy or completeness of the Content published herein and do not make any representations or warranties of any kind, express or implied, including but not limited to the implied warranties of merchantability, fitness for a particular purpose. The Publisher and Editor shall not be liable whatsoever for any errors, omissions, whether such errors or omissions result from negligence, accident, or any other cause or claims for loss or damages of any kind, including without limitation, indirect or consequential loss or damage arising out of use, inability to use, or about the reliability, accuracy or sufficiency of the information contained in this book.

ਮਨੁ ਜੀਤੇ ਜਗੁ ਜੀਤਿਆ ਜਾਂ ਤੇ ਬਿਖਿਆ ਤੇ ਹੋਇ ਉਦਾਸੁ ॥੨॥

man jee_tay jag jee_ti-aa jaa^N _tay bi_khi-aa _tay ho-ay u_daas.

Conquering the mind, one conquers the world and then remains detached from corruption.

CONTENTS

About the Author v
Foreword viii
Wishy's Magical Awakening xi
Success: A Word that Symbolizes Enthusiasm,
Admiration, and Dreams of a Better Future xiv

1. Demystifying – Defining Success 1
2. Mastering the Mind Maze – The Role of the Mindset 9
3. Soaring High Despite Failure – Accepting
   Failure as a Stepping Stone 18
4. Unbreakable Spirit, Unstoppable Success – Build
   Resilience 26
5. Gratitude and Appreciation 35
6. Build and Maintain Meaningful Relationships 43
7. Revealing the Path of Purpose – Finding
   Purpose and Meaning 51

Conclusion 60
From the Author 63
About Soft Skills Training 66
Voice of Clients 68
Acknowledgments 74

ABOUT THE AUTHOR

Gurpreet Kaur Chawla is a passionate and accomplished soft skills trainer with a deep-rooted commitment to empowering individuals to unlock their true potential. With a specialization in Communication Skills Training, she has enriched the lives of countless corporates and individuals alike.

Her journey as an expert communication skills and soft skills trainer began with a quest to understand the intricacies of successful communication in both personal and professional realms. Armed with a CELTA certification from Cambridge University and British Council, and as a NABET and SQA soft skills trainer and image consultant, Gurpreet embarked on a **mission** to equip individuals with the skills and confidence to excel in their language proficiency and interpersonal interactions.

Gurpreet is the visionary behind Abroadsify, an empowering brand that strives to make individuals "Abroad Ready" by training them to be well-rounded global citizens, ready to connect, communicate, and excel on the international stage.

She has been instrumental in transforming lives by enhancing communication abilities, fostering empathy, and building lasting connections based on the teachings of Gurbani.

Her expertise as an IELTS trainer has paved the way for more than 800 students to achieve exceptional success in their IELTS exams, opening doors to higher education and global opportunities.

Through her engaging training sessions and captivating workshops, Gurpreet has touched the lives of countless individuals by guiding them through the complexities of effective communication, and by inspiring them to embrace their unique journeys and redefine success on their own terms.

When Gurpreet isn't shaping lives through training, she can be found reading, meditating, or exploring the profound teachings of Gurbani. Her personal journey of self-discovery and growth continues to fuel her commitment to uplifting others, one heart at a time.

In "7 Things That Make You Love or Hate Success," Gurpreet invites you to embark on a transformative journey, unlocking the power of effective communication and redefining your path to success. Embrace her insights and practical guidance, and let her passion for empowering lives ignite the flame within you. As you navigate the unpredictable road to success, let Gurpreet be your guiding light, leading you to a life of purpose, fulfillment, and extraordinary achievements.

Let's follow her on Social Media:

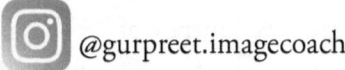 @gurpreet.imagecoach

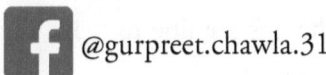 @gurpreet.chawla.31

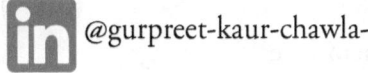 @gurpreet-kaur-chawla-

FOREWORD

Welcome to the transformative journey of "7 Things That Make You Love or Hate Success." As you embark on this enlightening adventure, here is a guide to make the most of your reading experience:

Dive into the Poetic Slice of Life

Begin your exploration with the intriguing poem that introduces you to the author's personal journey. Allow yourself to connect with the emotions and experiences shared, as it sets the stage for the captivating revelations that lie ahead.

Immerse Yourself in the Text

As you delve into the chapters, immerse yourself in the easy-to-understand language that blends profound wisdom and relatable anecdotes. Discover the factors that shape our perception of success and how you can redefine it on your own terms. Let each chapter ignite a spark of inspiration within you, urging you to embrace soft skills, resilience, and a growth mindset.

Engage in Meaningful Activities

Don't just read but actively participate in the practical activities provided in each chapter. These exercises are designed to help you introspect, develop emotional intelligence, and cultivate gratitude and appreciation in your daily life. Embrace these activities as opportunities for personal growth and self-discovery.

Reflect and Affirm

As you progress through the book, pause and reflect on the insights gained. Allow yourself to absorb the deep teachings and contemplate their significance in your life. Take time to ponder how you can apply these learnings to create a fulfilling and purpose-driven journey.

Before concluding each chapter, take a moment to recite the positive affirmations aloud. Affirmations are powerful tools that reinforce your beliefs and mindset. By speaking these affirmations out loud, you reinforce your commitment to embracing the key lessons shared in the book.

Remember, "7 Things That Make You Love or Hate Success" is not just a book but a transformative experience. It invites you to question your definition of success, embrace your uniqueness, and live a life that aligns with your true purpose. Let this guide lead you on a journey of self-mastery, empowering you to create a life filled with passion, contentment, and genuine success. Embrace each chapter with an open heart and mind, and let the magic of your transformation unfold.

Happy reading!

WISHY'S MAGICAL AWAKENING

Wishy! Wishy! Wishy!

Her name echoed through the air,

But deep within, she was unaware,

That her wishes were meant to be,

Guided by the power within, the real key.

Wishy's life was a thrilling ride,

A roller coaster with twists and turns,

But something within her yearned,

To understand who held the reins,

Of her destiny's majestic plains.

In her quest for meaning and success,

She stumbled upon a magical address,

A place where secrets were unveiled,

Where the illusion of control had paled.

The mysterious "I" stepped into view,

A player in the theater of her life,

Unseen, yet wielding power and strife,

It was time to confront this inner clue.

With every page she turned, a revelation,

The "I" was her mindset's creation,

A shape-shifter, often misled,

Defining success by what others said.

But a spark ignited deep inside,

As Wishy embarked on a magical ride,

To reclaim her power, to set it free,

To redefine success on her own decree.

Through challenges and self-discovery,

Wishy learned to decode the enigma,

To define success, her own schema,

To align with her values, with clarity.

No longer dictated by societal views,

She charted her path, her dreams she'd choose,

With newfound wisdom and fierce conviction,

Wishy embraced her unique mission.

This journey of self-discovery and more,

Would lead her to unlock success' door,

With each page turned, her spirit soared,

Her story, an adventure to be explored.

SUCCESS: A WORD THAT SYMBOLIZES ENTHUSIASM, ADMIRATION, AND DREAMS OF A BETTER FUTURE

We live in a world where achievements and awards are celebrated, and the concept of success is glorified. From an early age, we are taught to strive for success and see it as happiness, fulfillment, and accomplishment. We strive for success, driven by ambition and the belief that achieving our goals will bring us the ultimate satisfaction we desire.

However, real-world success often falls short of expectations. Even after reaching milestones, acquiring material wealth, or gaining social recognition, we still feel a void within. Precisely, more than success is needed to guarantee lasting fulfillment or true satisfaction.

Success: A Word that Symbolizes Enthusiasm, Admiration, and Dreams...

This book delves into the deeper layers of success. It explores the soft skills essential to fully embracing and experiencing success. We go beyond traditional measures of performance to address the often-overlooked aspects that contribute to a more meaningful and overall sense of accomplishment.

We start by challenging the definition of success itself. Beyond the social expectations and cultural influences that shape our perceptions, what does it mean for us as individuals?

The first chapter, "Decoding the Enigma – Defining Success," examines different perspectives on success and the impact of external expectations on our definition of ourselves. We will recognize the importance of defining success by our own standards, aligning it with our values, and setting meaningful goals that bring us true fulfillment.

From there, we dive deep into the role of mindset in shaping our sense of accomplishment. In Mastering the Mind's Maze – The Role of Mindset, we will discover how we think, especially how we think about growth which greatly influences our ability to achieve and maintain success. We will explore techniques to cultivate a growth mindset, overcome self-limiting beliefs, and embrace challenges as opportunities for growth.

Failure: A word that often has a negative connotation.

But Chapter 3, "Fail Forward, Soar Higher – Seeing Failure as a Springboard," challenges the conventional view of failure. We will explore the concept of reformulating failure, recognizing that it is a natural part of the journey to success. We will also discover famous examples of people who turned failure into an opportunity for growth followed by how to learn valuable lessons from setbacks, develop resilience, and learn how to use failure as a catalyst for personal and professional growth and provide strategy.

The chapters that follow gives insight into the transformative power of gratitude and appreciation, the importance of building and maintaining meaningful relationships, and the profound effects of finding meaning and purpose in life.

Success is a journey, not a destination, that goes beyond superficial achievements and embraces growth, connection, and fulfillment.

As you turn the page and submerge yourself into the next chapter, remember that success is not an ultimate goal to be pursued but a way of life that encompasses the gamut of human experience. This exploration of soft skills will redefine success, foster personal growth, and will not only inspire but empower you to build a life of extraordinary fulfillment.

Let's embark on this journey together and tap into the incredible potential that lies within each of us.

CHAPTER 1

DEMYSTIFYING – DEFINING SUCCESS

*S*uccess is often seen as the pinnacle of our achievement, the ultimate goal we strive for in our personal and professional lives. However, the concept of success is not as simple as it sounds. Many factors, including social norms, personal beliefs, and cultural influences, have an impact on it. This chapter explores the challenges of success, the different perspectives that shape our understanding of them, and the importance of defining success in your own words.

Societal expectations and external pressures often influence our definition of success. From an early age, we are bombarded with messages about what success looks like. Prestigious jobs, high incomes, material possessions, and social prestige. These external indicators of success can lead us to be narrow-minded and limiting, causing us to pursue goals that may not align with our true aspirations and values.

To free yourself from the influence of external expectations, it's important to critically question your definition of success. You need to reflect on the messages you've received in your life so far about what success is.

Consider the source of this news. Was it family, friends, media, or cultural influences? Ask yourself, if these definitions align with your own values and aspirations.

Activity:
Identifying My Personal Definition of Success

Find a quiet place to think, grab a pen and paper, or you can open a blank document on your computer.

1. Brainstorm your personal values

Start by identifying your core values. What is really important to you? Write down a list of values that align with your beliefs and principles.

Examples include:

Integrity: Upholding honesty, ethics, and moral principles in all aspects of life.

Respect: Treating oneself and others with kindness, dignity, and consideration.

Excellence: Striving for high standards, continuous improvement, and personal growth.

Compassion: Showing empathy, understanding, and care for others.

Authenticity: Being true to oneself, embracing individuality, and living with integrity.

Balance: Seeking harmony and equilibrium between various areas of life.

Courage: Facing challenges, taking risks, and standing up for what is right.

Gratitude: Cultivating appreciation and thankfulness for life's blessings.

Empowerment: Supporting and empowering oneself and others to reach their full potential.

Collaboration: Valuing teamwork, cooperation, and collective efforts.

2. Think about your personal goals

Next, think about what you want to achieve or experience in life. Think beyond society's expectations and focus on what brings you joy and fulfillment. What are your passions, dreams, and goals? Write them down, dream big, and think outside the box.

3. Identify meaningful goals

Consider your values and aspirations and identify specific goals that meet your definition of success. These goals should reflect what truly matters to you and contribute to your overall sense of accomplishment. Divide them into short-term and long-term goals and make sure they are measurable, realistic, and personally meaningful.

After completing this activity, you will have taken a positive step towards defining success on your terms.

Remember, success is not a one-size-fits-all concept. It is very personal and unique to each individual. Your definition of success may change over time, but that's perfectly normal and natural. The key is continually aligning your goals and aspirations with your values to set yourself on the path to success.

In the next chapter, we will examine the mindsets and skills necessary to fully embrace and experience success, regardless of external expectations. By clarifying your definition of success and setting meaningful goals, you can lay the foundation for a fulfilling and authentic path to success that truly speaks to you.

POSITIVE AFFIRMATIONS

Decoding the Enigma – The Definition of Success

I define success on my own terms and align it with my values and aspirations.

My definition of success is unique and authentic to me.

I embrace my journey and celebrate my achievements, big and small.

I am worthy of success and deserve to experience it fully.

I respect myself and honor the journey of others, recognizing that success is not a competition but a personal journey.

EMBRACING THE MIND'S INFINITE BOUNDS

Oh, the mind, a vast expanse it seems,

Uncharted territory, the land of dreams,

Fixed or growth, the choice is ours to make,

As Wishy discovered, for her mind's sake.

From fixed, she broke free, embracing the new,

A mindset of growth, where possibilities grew,

Believing in herself, her potential untold,

Wishy's mind expanded, an unending threshold.

No longer limited by self-imposed bounds,

She faced challenges with resilience that astounds,

No longer fearing failure, she saw it anew,

A stepping stone, a chance to learn and pursue.

The untrained mind, the deceptive "I" inside,

It held her captive, with limitations it tried,

But as Wishy trained her mind, step by step,

She discovered true success, a secret well-kept.

CHAPTER 2

MASTERING THE MIND MAZE – THE ROLE OF THE MINDSET

*O*ur mindset plays an important role in shaping our sense of accomplishment. It influences how we perceive and respond to challenges, setbacks, and successes. Here, it is worth exploring the power of mindsets and look at the difference between a fixed mindset and a growth mindset.

We will discuss techniques for developing a growth mindset, overcoming self-limiting beliefs, and developing a resilience mindset.

1. Understand the power of thought

Our mindset is the lens through which we interpret the world and our experiences. It depends on whether you see challenges as opportunities for growth or as insurmountable obstacles. When you recognize the impact of your mindset, you can control your thoughts and beliefs and ultimately shape your path to success.

2. Fixed mindset and growth mindset

A fixed mindset is indicated by the belief that one's skills and intelligence are fixed traits, with little control over the growth potential.

A growth mindset, on the other hand, is the belief that our abilities can be developed through dedication, hard work, and learning from experience.

Understanding the differences between these mindsets is critical to developing a mindset that supports your path to success

3. Cultivate a growth spirit

Developing a growth mindset is a transformational process that requires self-awareness and conscious effort.

Here are some techniques for cultivating a growth mindset:

Harness the power of yet

Replace the sentence "I can't" with "I can't yet." This simple language switch will show you that growth and progress are possible with time and effort.

Accept the challenge

See challenges as opportunities for growth, not threats. Use them as opportunities to learn new skills, develop them, and expand your skills.

Learn from your mistakes

Do not worry; see failure as a stepping stone to success, not as a reflection of your abilities. Learn valuable lessons from your failures and use them to refine your approach.

4. Overcome self-limiting beliefs

Self-limiting beliefs can hinder our progress and prevent us from reaching our full potential.

To overcome these beliefs:

Challenge negative thoughts

Identify self-limiting beliefs and question, their validity. Replace every negative thought with a positive and empowering thought.

Redefine frustration

Don't view setbacks as personal failures but as temporary obstacles on your path to success. Focus on lessons learned and growth achieved.

Think about supportive people in your life

Remember the people who believe in your potential and encourage you to grow. Your positive influence on them can help you overcome self-limiting beliefs.

5. Encourage positive self-talk

Talking to ourselves can either enhance or undermine our confidence and success so give yourself positive talk often.

To encourage positive self-talk:

Practice self-compassion

Treat yourself with kindness and understanding, especially during difficult times. Encourage and support yourself as you would a dear friend.

Use affirmations

Create positive affirmations that align with your goals and values. Repeat these regularly to reinforce positive self-talk and encourage a resilient mindset.

Celebrate your achievements

Acknowledge and celebrate your successes, no matter how small. Acknowledge your progress and reinforce positive self-talk by acknowledging your growth and accomplishments.

Activity:

Mindset Check and Positive Self-talk Practice

1. Mindset check

Take a moment to reflect on your own thoughts. Think about a challenge or setback you faced recently. How did you perceive these experiences? Did you approach them with a growth mindset or a fixed mindset? Write down any observations or patterns you notice.

2. Practice positive self-talk

Select a specific goal or challenge you are facing. Write down three positive affirmations that support your growth and progress toward your goals. Repeat these affirmations quietly or out loud daily to encourage positive self-talk and build a resilient mindset.

Cultivating a growth-oriented mindset and cultivating positive self-talk empowers you to take challenges, overcome self-limiting beliefs, and walk your path to success with resilience and determination.

In the chapter coming next, we will delve deeper into the concept of resilience and explore strategies for developing and maintaining it so that you can bounce back from setbacks and keep moving forward on your path to success.

POSITIVE AFFIRMATIONS

Mastering the Mind Maze – The Role of Mindset

I have a growth mindset and believe in my ability to overcome challenges.

I embrace challenges as opportunities for growth and learning.

I am resilient and adaptable, capable of navigating any obstacles on my path.

I release self-limiting beliefs and embrace the limitless possibilities that lie before me.

I am in control of my mindset, and I choose to cultivate positivity and optimism.

FAILURE'S GIFT, A STEPPING STONE

Oh, failure, a companion on this journey of life,

A teacher in disguise, guiding through strife,

Wishy once feared, but now she understands,

That failure holds treasures, lessons in its hands.

Like a phoenix rising, she soared above,

Failure's grip no longer suffocating her love,

For within every setback, a silver lining revealed,

Strength and resilience, her spirit now sealed.

Wishy's journey, a testament so clear,

Failure's embrace, she no longer fears,

For in the depths of failure, she found,

The keys to success, where growth is crowned.

CHAPTER 3

SOARING HIGH DESPITE FAILURE – ACCEPTING FAILURE AS A STEPPING STONE

*F*ailure is an obstacle to success and is often seen as a source of disappointment and discouragement. But this chapter explores a different perspective that recognizes failure as a natural and valuable part of the path to success. We'll explore famous examples of people who turned failure into an opportunity for growth and discuss strategies for redefining failure, learning valuable lessons from setbacks, and building resilience.

1. Recognize that failure is a natural part of the journey

Failure is not a sign of incompetence or inadequacy but an inevitable part of the learning process. Through our failures, we gain valuable insights, refine our strategies, and grow as individuals. Recognizing that failure is a natural and necessary part of the journey helps us view setbacks in a more positive, growth-oriented way of thinking.

2. Famous examples of failure and growth

Throughout history, countless people have failed along the way to success. From Thomas Edison's many experiments before the invention of the light bulb, J.K. Rowling's rejection of Harry Potter before finding a publisher, these examples show how failure can act as a catalyst for growth and eventual success. This indicates whether reflecting on these stories can inspire us to redefine our own mistakes as opportunities for learning and growth.

3. Reframe your mistakes and learn valuable lessons from them

To view failure as a stepping stone to success, you can use the following strategies:

Change your perspective

Instead of viewing failure as a personal reflection of your abilities, view it as a valuable learning experience. Ask yourself, "What can I learn from this setback?" and focus on gaining lessons and insights.

Get feedback and reflection

Proactively seek feedback from trusted mentors and peers to gain different perspectives and insights into the reasons for failure. Engage in self-reflection and identify areas for improvement and growth.

Adopt a growth mindset

Adopt a growth mindset and understand that failure doesn't define you; it provides opportunities to learn, adapt, and improve. Be confident that your skills and abilities can be developed through hard work and perseverance.

4. Build resilience and use failure as a catalyst

Resilience is the wonderful ability to recover from setbacks, adapt to challenges, and keep moving forward. Promote resilience and use failure as a catalyst for growth.

Build a supportive network

Surround yourself with people who believe in your potential and provide support during difficult times. Ask them for advice and encouragement to bounce back from failure.

Practice self-compassion

Be kind to yourself when you face failure. Treat yourself with compassion and understanding, and recognize that setbacks are a natural part of your path to success.

Set SMART goals

Set specific, measurable, achievable, relevant, and time-bound goals to guide progress. Breaking big goals into smaller, manageable steps helps you measure progress and maintain momentum.

Activity:
Reorganize Mistakes and Learn Lessons from Them

1. Identify

Identify any failures or setbacks you've experienced recently. Write down your first thoughts and feelings about it.

2. Rephrase the error

Challenge your initial thoughts by reframing failure as a learning experience. List three specific lessons you can learn from setbacks.

3. Action plan

Based on the lessons learned, create an action plan outlining specific steps you can take to apply those lessons and move forward. Set realistic goals and set a timeline to track your progress.

By recognizing failure as a natural part of the journey, redefining setbacks, and learning valuable lessons from them, you can turn failure into a catalyst for personal and professional growth. Cultivating resilience helps you bounce back from failure and stay purposeful and focused on your path to success.

In the next chapter, we will explore the power of appreciation and gratitude to understand how these qualities enhance our sense of accomplishment and promote feelings of fulfillment and happiness.

POSITIVE AFFIRMATIONS

Failing Forward, Soaring Higher – Embracing Failure as a Stepping Stone

Failure is not the end; it is a stepping stone toward my growth and success.

I extract valuable lessons from setbacks and use them to propel myself forward.

I embrace failure as an opportunity for personal and professional development.

I am resilient and bounce back stronger after every setback.

I am grateful for the lessons learned through failure and remain open to new opportunities.

RESILIENCE, THE UNBREAKABLE SPIRIT

In the face of adversity, Wishy stood strong,

Her spirit unbreakable, resilience a lifelong song,

She weathered storms, withstood life's tests,

For her spirit, unyielding, gave her zest.

Stress may knock, but she refused to fall,

A warrior within, she answered the call,

With each challenge faced, her strength grew,

Resilience her shield, guiding her through.

Oh, unbreakable spirit, an unstoppable force,

Wishy soared high, her purpose set course,

Through the highs and lows, she persevered,

Resilience, her ally, her doubts disappeared.

CHAPTER 4

UNBREAKABLE SPIRIT, UNSTOPPABLE SUCCESS – BUILD RESILIENCE

*R*esilience is a fundamental trait that plays a key role in navigating the ups and downs on the road to success. This chapter delves into the importance of resilience and its importance in overcoming challenges and achieving sustained success. We will examine the characteristics of resilient people and discuss strategies for increasing emotional resilience, coping with stress, and staying motivated during difficult times. We will also explore how setbacks can be used as opportunities for growth.

1. Understand the importance of resilience

Resilience is the ability to adapt and recover from adversity. It is the trait that enables individuals to face setbacks and challenges with strength, determination, and unwavering spirit. Recognizing the importance of resilience will help you develop the skills you need to overcome obstacles and thrive.

2. Characteristics of resilient people

Resilient people possess certain key qualities that contribute to their ability to bounce back from adversity. They are as follows:

Emotional control

Resilient people can effectively manage their emotions and maintain balance even in difficult situations.

Optimism and positive outlook

Resilient people maintain a positive attitude and focus on opportunities and solutions rather than dealing with setbacks.

Adaptability and flexibility

Resilient people can embrace change, adapt to new situations, and adjust their approach when obstacles are encountered.

3. Build emotional resilience

Emotional resilience is key to staying motivated and managing stress during difficult times.

Strategies for building emotional resilience include:

Develop confidence

Gain a deeper understanding of your emotions, triggers, and coping mechanisms. Practice introspection and mindfulness to develop emotional awareness.

Find support

Build a support system of friends, family, and mentors who can provide guidance, encouragement, and listening during difficult times.

Develop a coping strategy

Identify healthy coping mechanisms that help you manage stress and build emotional resilience. Examples of this include playing sports, journaling, meditating, and pursuing hobbies.

4. Cope with stress and stay motivated

Stress and lack of motivation can stunt your progress and undermine your success.

To manage stress and stay motivated:

Prioritize self-care

Maintain your physical and mental health by getting enough sleep, nourishing yourself, and participating in activities that bring you joy and relaxation.

Break down tasks into manageable steps

When you face an overwhelming challenge, break it down into smaller, achievable tasks. This approach helps keep you motivated and gives you a sense of progress.

Set realistic goals

Set challenging but achievable goals. Celebrate small wins along the way to stay motivated and keep the momentum going.

5. Use setbacks as opportunities for growth

Resilient people see setbacks as opportunities for growth and learning.

To use setbacks:

Reframe error

See setbacks as learning experiences and opportunities for personal and professional growth. Analyze what went wrong, identify lessons learned, and apply them in the future.

Practice self-compassion

Be kind and understanding to yourself when you face setbacks. Give yourself the same compassion and encouragement you would give a friend in a similar situation.

Activity:

Promote Resilience and Manage Stress

1. Think

Think about your current difficult situation and any setbacks you've experienced. Write down relevant feelings, thoughts, and actions.

2. Identify strategy

Based on the strategies described in this chapter, we identify three specific techniques that you can use to increase your emotional resilience and manage stress in similar situations in the future.

3. Action plan

Create an action plan outlining how you will incorporate these strategies into your daily life. Set measurable goals and establish routines to support your resilience-building efforts.

By building resilience, managing stress, and staying motivated during difficult times, you'll have the tools you need to overcome obstacles and stay on your path to success. Seeing setbacks as opportunities for growth, cultivating an unbreakable spirit, and leading to unstoppable success.

In the next chapter, we will explore the transformative power of appreciation and gratitude and how these qualities can enhance our overall well-being and deepen our sense of accomplishment.

POSITIVE AFFIRMATIONS

Unbreakable Spirit, Unstoppable Success – Developing Resilience

I am strong and resilient, capable of facing any challenges that come my way.

I manage stress with grace and maintain a positive outlook during difficult times.

I stay focused on my goals and motivated even when faced with obstacles.

I am in control of my emotions and choose to respond to challenges with resilience and determination.

I embrace setbacks as opportunities for growth and emerge stronger than ever before.

GRATITUDE'S EMBRACE, A HEART ALIGHT

In the depths of gratitude, Wishy found,

A treasure trove, where joy did abound,

Her heart alight, with thankfulness it soared,

Appreciating life's blessings, big and small, she adored.

With open arms, she embraced each day,

Gratitude's magic, lighting her way,

For in the simplest of moments, she discovered,

The beauty of life, love's embrace uncovered.

Oh, gratitude, a companion so dear,

Wishy's heart filled, joy drawing near,

In gratitude's embrace, she found peace,

A blissful release, where worries cease.

CHAPTER 5

GRATITUDE AND APPRECIATION

$\mathcal{G}$ratitude is a powerful emotion that transforms our sense of accomplishment and increases not only our mental well-being but promotes happiness throughout life. This chapter explores the role of gratitude in experiencing and maintaining success. We will examine the positive impact of gratitude on our mental and emotional state and share practical tips and exercises to encourage gratitude and recognition in our daily lives.

1. Gratitude's role in experiencing and maintaining success

Gratitude allows us to recognize and appreciate the positive aspects of our lives, such as our achievements, relationships, and personal growth. It shifts our focus from what we lack to what we already have, promoting feelings of fulfillment. By cultivating gratitude, one can increase and sustain their successes in the long run.

2. Gratitude positively impacts mental health

Gratitude is associated with various mental and emotional benefits. Research shows that practicing gratitude regularly can help you:

Improve your overall luck

Expressing gratitude lifts your mood and increases your overall sense of well-being and happiness.

Reduce stress and anxiety

Gratitude helps distract attention from negative thoughts and worries, reducing stress and anxiety.

Promote resilience

Cultivating gratitude strengthens our ability to cope with adversity and bounce back from setbacks and build resilience in the face of adversity.

3. Practical tips for developing gratitude

Keep a gratitude journal

Take a few minutes each day and write down three things that you are grateful for. Think about the positive aspects of your day, no matter how small. This exercise will help you focus on gratitude and train your mind to seek out the positive.

Be mindful and grateful

Stop and enjoy the moment during your daily activities, such as eating or even taking a walk. Notice and appreciate the sights, sounds, tastes, and sensations. Cultivate an appreciation for life's small pleasures.

Express gratitude to others

Take time to express your gratitude to those around you in your life. Write a heartfelt thank you letter, send a thank you email, or simply send a verbal thank you note. Acknowledging the contributions of others fosters deeper connections and increases mutual appreciation.

Practice gratitude even in difficult situations

When faced with difficulties or setbacks, consciously look for the bright spots and lessons from the experience. Look for opportunities for personal growth and show gratitude for the resilience and strength you have developed.

4. Gratitude meditation exercise

Participating in gratitude meditation deepens gratitude.

Here are some really simple exercises you can include in your daily routine.

Find a quiet, comfortable place. Close your eyes and take a few deep breaths to focus on yourself.

Remind yourself of three things you are grateful for right now. These may be simple aspects of your life, or they may be important ones.

Focus on each point and let the gratitude flow from it. Fully experience and appreciate the positive emotions that accompany each gratitude.

Stay in this gratitude space for a few minutes and enjoy the feeling of gratitude and abundance.

Activity:

Weekly Gratitude Reflection Exercise

Reflecting on your week can help you develop a practice of gratitude.

Try the following exercises:

Take a few minutes each week to reflect on positive moments and experiences you've had.

Write down three things you are grateful for that relate specifically to the week you are thinking about.

Take your time enjoying and evaluating each item on the list. Think about the positive impact it has had on your life and express your gratitude for it.

By incorporating these practical tips and practices into your daily life, you can cultivate appreciation and recognition as an integral part of your thinking. Harness the power of gratitude to increase your overall well-being, deepen your sense of accomplishment, and live a more fulfilling and joyful life.

In the next chapter, we will explore the importance of building and maintaining meaningful relationships on our path to success and understand how connecting with others contributes to our overall well-being.

POSITIVE AFFIRMATIONS

Gratitude and Appreciation

I am grateful for the abundant blessings in my life, and I express my gratitude daily.

I appreciate the beauty in every moment and find joy in the simplest of things.

I cultivate a grateful heart, which attracts positivity and abundance into my life.

I embrace gratitude as a transformative practice that enhances my overall well-being.

I am open to receiving and expressing gratitude, spreading its ripple effect to those around me.

BUILDING BRIDGES, NURTURING CONNECTIONS

In the tapestry of life, relationships intertwine,

Wishy wove bonds, hearts aligned,

Through kindness and respect, connections grew,

Building bridges, her love ever true.

With open ears and compassionate eyes,

She listened, understood, empathized,

In nurturing relationships, she found,

A support system, love's sacred ground.

Oh, meaningful connections, so profound,

Wishy discovered, hearts can truly astound,

For in building bridges, she realized,

The power of love, where souls harmonize.

CHAPTER 6

BUILD AND MAINTAIN MEANINGFUL RELATIONSHIPS

*W*hen striving for success, we often focus on personal achievements and personal goals. But success is not just about individual efforts. The relationships we form and maintain along the way play an important role in our overall well-being and fulfillment. This chapter explores the importance of relationships for success and examines how meaningful connections contribute to our well-being. It also provides amazing strategies for building and maintaining supportive relationship networks.

1. The importance of relationships in success

Success is not an isolated journey. Meaningful relationships can bring a sense of belonging, support, and encouragement, facilitate our progress, and increase our overall well-being. Relationships bring joy, connection, and purpose to our lives and give depth and meaning to our accomplishments.

2. How meaningful connections contribute to happiness and fulfilment

Meaningful relationships have a huge impact on our happiness and fulfillment. Here are some of the ways they contribute:

Emotional support

A trusting relationship provides a safe space for sharing successes, challenges, and weaknesses. They provide emotional support, empathy, and understanding in both successes and setbacks.

Motivation and responsibility

Meaningful connections serve as a source of motivation and accountability. Surrounding ourselves with people who share our values and ambitions inspires us to strive for greatness and stay true to our goals.

Collaboration and networking

Building relationships with like-minded people opens doors to collaboration and opportunity. Meaningful connections create a supportive network that can provide guidance, mentorship, and valuable insights on your path to success.

3. Strategies for building and maintaining supportive relationships

Trust and vulnerability

Be sincere, show vulnerability, and speak openly about your experiences, dreams, and challenges. This builds trust and deepens bonds.

Active listening and empathy

Practice active listening by being present and paying attention when interacting with others. Show empathy by trying to understand their perspectives, experiences, and feelings. By truly listening to their opinions and valuing their insights, you develop a deeper connection.

Giving and receiving

Maintain a balanced dynamic in your relationships. Offer support, encouragement, and assistance when needed, and be open to helping others. Embrace the reciprocity of relationships and the power of giving and receiving.

Promote common interests

Look for opportunities to engage in activities and pursuits that match your interests. Join groups, clubs, and organizations where you can meet people who share your passion. These shared interests provide a strong foundation for meaningful connections.

Maintain relationships

Relationships require effort and investment. Take time to stay in touch with the people who are important to you. Schedule regular check-ins, reach out with genuine interest and care, and strive to nurture those contacts.

Activity:

Reflection and Action Practice

Reflect on your current relationships.

Consider the quality of existing relationships. Identify what brings you joy, support, and fulfillment and what is harmful and draining.

Identify growth areas

Identify gaps and areas for improvement in your relationship-building efforts. Are there specific qualities or skills you would like to develop to improve your relationships with others?

Take proactive measures

Based on reflection, set goals and take actionable steps to build and maintain meaningful relationships. This may include contacting old friends, joining social groups, or attending classes to improve your communication skills.

Recognizing the importance of relationships to success and implementing strategies to build and maintain meaningful connections will build a supportive network that will propel you forward. Harness the power of relationships to promote happiness, fulfillment, and lasting success.

The next chapter delves into the deeper implications of finding meaning and purpose in life and how aligning personal values and goals can create greater fulfillment and satisfaction on the journey to success. We will understand what we can do.

POSITIVE AFFIRMATIONS

Building and Maintaining Meaningful Relationships

I cultivate meaningful connections and foster nourishing relationships in my life.

I treat myself and others with kindness, respect, and empathy.

I attract positive and supportive people who uplift and inspire me.

I communicate effectively and listen with empathy and understanding.

I value the diversity and uniqueness of others, fostering an environment of acceptance and love.

PURPOSE'S CALLING, A LIFE REBORN

In the quest for purpose, Wishy found,

A calling deep within, her soul's resound,

She aligned her values, let passion lead,

A life reborn, fulfilling every need.

Oh, purpose, a guiding light so bright,

Wishy embraced it, her heart alight,

In purpose's embrace, she discovered,

A profound fulfillment, where dreams were uncovered.

Each day a canvas, purpose her guide,

Living with enthusiasm, no longer tied,

To societal notions, she carved her own way,

Believing in herself, in every word she'd say.

CHAPTER 7

REVEALING THE PATH OF PURPOSE – FINDING PURPOSE AND MEANING

*S*uccess is not defined solely by external achievements or material possessions. It goes hand in hand with finding meaning and purpose in life. This final chapter explores the deep connection between success and purpose, discovering your personal values and techniques for aligning them with your professional goals. We emphasize the importance of embedding purpose into our daily actions and decisions and offer strategies for adopting a purpose-driven mindset that leads to a deep sense of accomplishment.

1. The link between success and finding meaning in life

True success goes beyond surface performance metrics. It is inseparable from finding meaning and purpose in our efforts. When you align your actions with your values and passions, you tap into a deeper source of motivation and fulfillment.

2. Discover your personal values and align them with your professional goals

To find meaning, it's important to understand our core values and align them with our professional aspirations. Here are some techniques to help with this process:

Self-reflection

Take time for introspection and self-discovery. Find your passions, interests, and values that drive you. Consider how these align with your career goals.

Identify core values

Determine your core values and prioritize these values in your decision-making.

Purposeful goal setting

Set meaningful, purpose-driven goals that align with your values.

3. Integrate goals into daily actions and decisions

Living a goal-oriented life requires consciously incorporating goals into your daily actions and decisions.

Strategies to facilitate this integration include:

Conscious adjustments

Evaluate regularly whether your actions and decisions are aligned with your values and goals. To stay on track, consciously introspect.

Set priorities

Identify key areas of focus and devote time and energy to activities that align with your goals. Prioritize tasks that contribute to an overall sense of purpose and fulfillment.

Make targeted decisions

Consider the potential impact your decisions can have on your values and goals. Make decisions that align with your long-term vision and goals, even if it means sacrificing or stepping out of your comfort zone.

Adopt a goal-oriented mindset and experience a sense of accomplishment

Purposeful thinking lays a strong foundation for lasting success and deep fulfillment.

Here's how to cultivate and embrace this mindset:

Embrace growth and learning

Adopt a continuous growth and learning mindset and look for opportunities to develop and expand your skills on purpose.

Finding meaning in challenges

View challenges as great opportunities for growth and learning. Consider them essential steps on your path to success and purpose.

Practice gratitude and appreciation

Develop an appreciation for journeys and opportunities that match your destination. Appreciate the progress you've made and the positive impact you're having on others.

Celebrate milestones and impact

Celebrate your accomplishments, big and small, and the positive impact you're making on others and the world around you. Acknowledge the meaningful contributions you make to your work and relationships.

Activity:

Reflection and Action Practice

Think about your goals.

Take time to reflect and think about the meaning of your life. What are your core values, passions, and long-term goals? Write a personal mission statement that summarizes your goals.

Set purposeful goals

Align your goals with your purpose. Identify specific actions and steps you can take to move closer to your goals. Create a roadmap to reach your goals.

Act with intent

Work on building your goals into your daily actions. Consider whether your decisions and actions are aligned with your goals and values. Make conscious adjustments and make purposeful decisions.

Understanding the relationship between success and goals, aligning your personal values with your professional goals, incorporating your goals into your daily actions, and adopting a goal-oriented mindset will unlock a deep sense of accomplishment and lasting success. Be guided by your purpose and live each day with it, shaping your path to a meaningful life.

Overall, this book explores our experiences of success, from defining success in our own words to accepting failure, developing resilience, cultivating gratitude, building meaningful relationships, and finding meaning. We explored seven key aspects that influence, and by incorporating these principles into our lives, we surely can embark on a transformational journey towards success that is holistic, fulfilling, and aligned with who we really are.

POSITIVE AFFIRMATIONS

Unveiling the Path of Purpose – Finding Purpose and Meaning

I am connected to my inner purpose, and my actions align with my true calling.

My life has profound meaning and significance, as I embrace my unique purpose.

I am guided by my values and passions, creating a life of purpose and fulfillment.

I trust in the unfolding of my journey, knowing that every experience serves a higher purpose.

I live each day with a deep sense of purpose, making a positive impact on the world around me.

THE AWAKENING WITHIN

In the depths of Wishy's journey, she found,

That the untrained mind held her bound,

But step by step, she rewrote her fate,

Training her mind, embracing a new state.

True success, she realized, was not far,

It resided within, beneath every scar,

Living each day with enthusiasm and zest,

Acceptance, belief, kindness, and being the best.

As Wishy's story concludes, dear reader, take heed,

Unleash the power within, the change you need,

For in training your mind, a transformation awaits,

A life of true success, where joy resonates.

Believe in yourself, for you hold the key,

To unlock the potential that yearns to be free,

Embrace respect, kindness, positivity too,

And witness the magic as your dreams come true.

The journey continues, your story unfolds,

With each page turned, new chapters behold,

May the lessons of Wishy's quest inspire your way,

To a life of meaning and success, starting today.

CONCLUSION

*E*mbrace the journey and embody extraordinary success.

Let me close this book by stressing the importance of incorporating these soft skills and mindsets into your pursuit of success. Success is not defined solely by external achievements. It is a comprehensive and multifaceted journey. It requires defining success by your own standards, cultivating mindset and resilience, cultivating gratitude and meaningful relationships, and finding meaning in your actions. By embodying these qualities, we can face life's inevitable ups and downs with grace and celebrate truly extraordinary successes. Everyone's path to success is different, and following your own path is important. Don't compare yourself to others or be influenced by external standards of success. Instead, let us define success based on our own values, passions, and aspirations. We create a fulfilling, meaningful, and authentic life by aligning our goals with who we are.

As you close this book, take time to reflect on the lessons learned, the practices you have put into practice, and

Conclusion

the principles you have explored. Consider how you can incorporate these concepts into your daily life to continue your personal journey to extraordinary success. Embrace the process, celebrate your progress, and know that true success lies not just in your goals but in the growth and change you experience along the way.

May you embark on a journey of purpose, resilience, gratitude, meaningful connections, and a deep sense of accomplishment. Embody extraordinary success and shine your own light on the world.

Conclusion

FINAL POSITIVE AFFIRMATIONS

I am deserving of success, happiness, and fulfillment in all areas of my life.

I trust in my own abilities and believe in my limitless potential to create the life I desire.

I am grateful for every opportunity and experience that comes my way, as they contribute to my growth and evolution.

I choose to embrace challenges as stepping stones toward personal and professional development.

I am the author of my own story, and I have the power to create a life that is extraordinary and aligned with my true purpose.

FROM THE AUTHOR

Dear Readers,

I stand before you not only as an author but as a passionate advocate for embracing success on your own terms. Through the pages of this book, I have delved into the intricacies of what truly defines success and how it can be experienced in its purest form. As I share the insights and wisdom gathered over years of study and personal growth, I urge you, dear parents, students, and everyone, to embark on a journey of self-discovery and redefine success on your terms.

To Parents

As parents, you hold the key to nurturing the next generation of visionaries and dreamers. I implore you to let your children define success on their terms, to guide them by the side rather than imposing your aspirations on them. Each child is born with unique talents, passions, and dreams, and it is by allowing them the freedom to explore and embrace these gifts that they will truly flourish. Be the guiding light, supporting them through the ups and downs of life, and instilling in them the values of resilience, empathy, and compassion. Your unwavering belief in their potential will empower them to shine as they tread the path to their own version of success.

To Students

Dear students, success is not a one-size-fits-all journey. As you step into the world of possibilities and opportunities, take a moment to clearly define success for yourself. Understand that it is not merely about accolades or material achievements but rather about discovering your passions and making a positive impact on the world. Embrace your uniqueness and remember that each failure is an opportunity to learn and grow. Set meaningful goals, fuelled by your dreams, and let perseverance be your companion in this magnificent voyage. As you embark on your path to success, know that the power to shape your destiny lies within you.

To Everyone

Success is not an isolated destination but a continuous journey that evolves with every step we take. To everyone reading this, I urge you to pause and reflect on what success truly means to you. Let go of societal pressures and external expectations, and instead, embrace your own truth and values. Success, in its most authentic form, is about living a life that resonates with your passions, values, and purpose. It is about finding joy and contentment in the pursuit of your dreams. Let this book be a reminder that you have the power to redefine success and create a life that is extraordinary and uniquely yours.

Remember, you are capable of greatness, and success is but a reflection of the greatness within you.

With warm regards,

Gurpreet Kaur Chawla

ABOUT SOFT SKILLS TRAINING

*S*oft skills **include personal skills, social skills, communication skills, personality** traits, **attitudes,** and **ways of thinking,** as well as **the combination of** social and emotional **qualities** which are sought for in all professions.

A Soft Skills Trainer (on one or all of the below areas, to individuals or groups):

- Guides on a journey of **self-discovery and personal growth,** helping you uncover your strengths and areas for improvement.
- Enhances **communication skills,** both verbal and written, to enable clear and effective expression of ideas.
- Teaches **conflict resolution techniques,** fostering better relationships and collaboration in various settings.

- Develops **emotional intelligence,** empowering you to understand and manage emotions for improved interactions.
- Provides **leadership development training,** equipping you with the skills to inspire and lead teams effectively.
- Conducts **team-building** activities, fostering trust and cooperation within groups to enhance overall performance.
- Offers **stress management** tools and coping strategies to maintain a healthy work-life balance.
- Teaches practical **time management** techniques to prioritize tasks and boost productivity.
- Guides you on **networking skills,** helping you build and nurture professional relationships for career growth.
- Enhances **problem-solving and critical thinking abilities,** enabling you to tackle challenges with confidence.

If you or someone known to you feels the need for soft skills training for themselves or their companies, I can be reached on my email **abroadsify@gmail.com**

www.abroadsify.com

VOICE OF CLIENTS

Source: Linked in Posts by learners

- I am delighted to announce that I have completed a Value added course from "COLLEGE TO CORPORATE"

  I embarked on this journey, with dreams and aspirations, and a burning desire to transition from the world of academia to the realm of the corporate world.

  Throughout this course, I have not only gained invaluable knowledge and skills but have also developed my character and grown as an individual. I have learned the importance of teamwork, communication, and adaptability. I have embraced the art of problem-solving and critical thinking. And most importantly, I have acquired the ability to constantly learn and evolve in a rapidly changing professional landscape.

  I want to express my deepest gratitude to our esteemed faculty members and Gurpreet Kaur Chawla ma'am who have tirelessly guided us students at DIAS with their wisdom and expertise through this course. Their dedication and commitment to our growth have been instrumental in shaping us into professionals. We owe them a debt of gratitude for igniting the fire within us and for helping us navigate the path from college to corporate life.

This is just the beginning of a lifelong journey of learning and growth.

- I just want to say thank you for helping me achieve the desired score. It looked like an impossible task to score well in all the modules of IELTS General Training test but it happened with your support and guidance. You have been an amazing teacher who always motivated me to perform better.

  The way you teach is commendable.

  Especially the speaking practice sessions with Gurpreet Ma'am helped me in building up my confidence for the exam.

  I would strongly recommend Abroadsify's crash course to learn the tips and tricks which really helped me.

- Here is a glimpse of 30 hours value added course organized by our college.

  Completing an immersive corporate readiness course at our college was an incredible journey of learning and hands-on activities. From immersive learning to hands-on activities, it paved the way for a successful transition into the corporate world. Grateful for the invaluable skills and knowledge gained along this remarkable journey.

Special Thanks to Gurpreet Kaur Chawla for guiding us all through this corporate readiness course. Your guidance and expertise made our corporate-ready course truly exceptional.

- The session was conducted on ABC of Image building. Special thanks to Gurpreet Kaur Chawla for her guidance throughout the session.

  We gained insights into the art of projecting a winning image that is Appropriate (Style Scale and clothing messages), Authentic (Yin and Yang), Attractive (Body Shape, Personal Colouring, Face Shape, grooming) and Affordable (Clustering) understood and demonstrated through fun activities and group presentations based on 8 piece professional cluster PPT creation.

  During the session, I learned a great deal about: Appearance Management, behavior, and communication.

  Overall, the session was informative and effective management of your appearance, behavior, and communication skills can help you make a positive impression on others, build strong relationships, and achieve your personal and professional goals.

- It has been an invaluable learning experience, and I wanted to outline the key takeaways I have gained from your teachings.

Firstly, I am incredibly grateful for the insights and strategies you shared regarding goal-setting and goal-getting. Your emphasis on setting specific, measurable, achievable, relevant, and time-bound (SMART) goals has revolutionized my approach to personal and professional aspirations. By learning to break down larger goals into smaller, actionable steps, I now feel more confident and equipped to pursue my objectives effectively.

The section on cultural competence and networking was truly eye-opening. Your explanations of different cultural practices and communication styles have broadened my understanding of global business environments. I now possess a heightened awareness of the importance of cultural sensitivity and adaptability, which I believe will greatly benefit me in future professional interactions. The networking techniques you shared, such as active listening and building genuine connections, have empowered me to establish valuable relationships and expand my professional network.

The exploration of emotional intelligence and resilience was another significant highlight of the course. Understanding the various facets of emotional intelligence, such as self-awareness, self-regulation, empathy, and relationship management, has helped me cultivate a more balanced and harmonious approach to both personal and professional relationships. Additionally, the strategies and tools you provided to enhance resilience have equipped me to navigate challenges with a positive mindset and bounce back stronger from setbacks.

Lastly, the section on the ABC of image management was incredibly insightful. Learning about the impact of professional attire, grooming, body language, and effective communication skills on one's personal brand has been transformative. I now appreciate the importance of making a positive and lasting impression, and I feel more confident in presenting myself professionally in various corporate settings.

Once again, I would like to express my heartfelt appreciation for Ms. Gurpreet Kaur Chawla

- I had a great experience learning at Abroadsify. IELTS classes with Gurpreet Ma'am not only helped me to improve the structure of the writing tasks but to gain insights into how to write more effectively. The speaking classes helped me to become a lot more confident person. Thank you for helping and guiding me. It would not have been possible without your efforts to score 7.5 in the first go.
- Hello ma'am, I'm finally leaving and going to Australia to pursue my master's. Studied for IELTS back in October 2021 and ma'am it was such a wonderful and enriching experience, really.

I had so many milestones and each one of them reminded me of you and what tips you used to give when I was attending your lectures apart from my IELTS preparation.

I graduated, gave interviews for University enrolment, endless job interviews as I had some time in hand before admission, and finally got into a job too. All of them required conversing in English and made me revisit what I learned then.

Never did I ever think I'll take something that I learned from an examination point of view this far in life. And you're all I can thank for the same.

Your student is finally leaving for adding another milestone to the set. Thank you for being a part of my life, ma'am.

And many more……..

ACKNOWLEDGMENTS

$\mathcal{F}$irst and foremost, I express my heartfelt thanks to the Almighty for blessing me with the most incredible support system. I am truly grateful for my loving parents, powerful mentors, supportive husband, and my precious children, who have been my pillars of strength throughout this journey.

To my parents, Mr. Hardev Singh Saluja and Mrs. Kawaljeet Kaur Saluja, thank you for your unconditional love and valuable life lessons. From my father, I learned the virtues of discipline and consistency, while my mother instilled in me the essence of networking and creativity.

My heartfelt gratitude goes to my in-laws, Late Mrs. Davinder Kaur Chawla and Mr. Satnam Singh Chawla, who embraced me as their own and supported me wholeheartedly since my marriage at the age of 18.5 years. To my sister-in-law, Mrs. Mandeep Kaur Chawla, and brother-in-law, Mr. Bhupinder Singh Chawla, thank you for treating me like your younger sister and being a constant source of love and care.

Acknowledgments

I am immensely blessed to have my adorable children, Master Abner Singh Chawla and Master Guransh Singh Chawla, as well as my niece, Miss Jasleen Kaur Chawla and nephew, Master Harshdeep Singh Chawla in my life. They are my inspiration and motivation to practice and impart soft skills with full dedication.

To my dear husband, Mr. Maninder Singh Chawla, your unwavering belief in me and my work has been my driving force. Your support and encouragement have been my greatest strength, and I am grateful beyond words.

I extend my heartfelt thanks to my dear friends, colleagues, students and everyone who contributed to the creation of this book and made this journey remarkable.

To my mentors, Mr. Ganesh Dalvi, Mr. Rakesh Agarwal, Mrs. Suman Agarwal, Mrs. Renu Mehra and Inspiring Jatin, I am indebted to your guidance, wisdom, and motivation. Your mentorship has shaped my thoughts and ideas, and I consider myself blessed to have learned from you.

I am also thankful to all the individuals and professionals who generously shared their time and insights during the research process. Your expertise and contributions have enriched the content of this book.

Lastly, to you, the readers, thank you for being a part of this incredible journey. Your interest and engagement with my work give meaning and purpose to what I do. I hope the insights and knowledge shared in this book bring value to your life.

With deepest gratitude,

Gurpreet Kaur Chawla
Director, Abroadsify
www.abroadsify.com
abroadsify@gmail.com

www.ingramcontent.com/pod-product-compliance
Lightning Source LLC
LaVergne TN
LVHW041625070526
838199LV00052B/3240